How To
DEADLIFT 600 LBS.
RAW

12-Week Deadlift Program
&
Technique Guide

By
Ryan J. Mathias

MathiasMethod.com

COPYRIGHT

DISCLAIMER

ABOUT THE AUTHOR

Ryan J. Mathias

Hi,

I'm Ryan Mathias, creator of the Mathias Method Strength System and for years I have been helping people all over the world, from total beginners to elite athletes, learn how to get stronger, perform better, and achieve their goals.

As an athlete, Strength Coach and competitive Powerlifter with 10+ years of experience, all backed by a Degree in Exercise Science, I have taken my experience and combined it with my education to bring you the best and most effective knowledge available.

I share everything I know in my books and it is my goal to help as many people as I can learn how to achieve their goals. Because I measure my success not by how many books I sell, but by how many people I help.

So, if you want to learn how to get bigger, stronger, faster, and overall perform better, then I'm your guy!

Plus, if you ever have any questions, you can email me anytime and I will do my best to help you reach your goals!

Email: ryan@mathiasmethod.com
I would love to hear from you!

Join me on Social Media: @RyanJMathias

BOOKS BY RYAN J. MATHIAS

   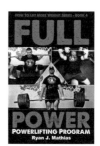

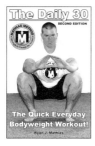   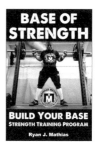

Available on

Amazon.com

and

StrengthWorld.store

Dedication

This information is dedicated to you, the lifter. To those of you that believe in becoming stronger. Stronger through self-improvement and the pursuit of greater achievement. For those that always push for more and crave success every day. For those that don't let challenges stop them from doing what they set out to do. For all the dreamers out there, that keep their dreams alive!

This information is dedicated to YOU, because YOU are the only one that can make a difference in your life. YOU are the only one that can change YOUR world!

Thank You

Thank you to all those that read this information and use it to help others. My mission is to help as many people as I can change the world through strength and I know I can't do it alone. So, thank you for standing with me.

TABLE OF CONTENTS

PART 1

INTRODUCTION

A Note From The Author

Hey Lifter!

I hope you are ready to get really strong, because you are about to embark on an incredible Strength Journey! The same journey that I followed when I first started! The journey to get stronger!

Now, back in 2012 I broke my back. I had a crushed vertebra (T11) and two bulged discs. No, it was not from weight lifting. It was a sport related injury. However, I believe that my lifting did have an indirect impact on my injury, because I was doing it all wrong.

I was going too heavy too often and lifting with bad form. All I wanted was to get stronger and I was fighting as hard as I could to reach my goals. It just wasn't working out.

As it turned out, breaking my back was actually one of the best things that ever happened to me, because it gave me time to start over. I was able to look back at my mistakes, learn from them, and become a beginner again.

I started back perfecting the technique of all my lifts, learning how the pros did it, and slowly progressed back towards my goals. Now, my back is stronger and feels better than it ever has!

I learned so much during my time off and during that entire year of rebuilding myself that I became more obsessed with strength than ever before!

I used to be stuck at a 500lb. deadlift max before my back injury, but after learning how to deadlift properly and train smarter, I took my deadlift to 600+lbs. in a matter of months!

However, it wasn't easy for me to get there. I had to work hard for it! Which is why I made this book. To give you an easier path to reach that almost seemingly unattainable goal of finally deadlifting 600+ lbs. totally RAW!

In fact, I created the entire *How To Lift More Weight* series for all the Strength Warriors out there that are just like us, looking to get stronger! I really want to help others, achieve their goals of lifting as much weight as they can dream of in all their lifts!

Just remember, it won't be easy. You are gonna have to work for it. I am giving you all the tools you need to succeed, but the rest is up to you.

Before you get started, I want you to realize that no ordinary person has ever completed this Journey. That is because in order to reach such an incredible strength feat, you cannot be ordinary. You have to develop yourself into someone that has character, focus and strength beyond the ordinary. You will have to become extraordinary in your efforts to defeat the challenging road that lays ahead.

You will have to be consistent, dedicated and self-disciplined enough to persevere to the end. You can have others join in along your journey, but YOU must be the one that keeps fighting until the end. No one can do it for you. You have to be the one that decides to not give up and push on no matter how hard it gets.

I cannot promise that you will reach your goal, but I will guarantee that this program will guide you as far as you want to go. The rest is up to you. Are you ready?

Strength To You,

Ryan J. Mathias

Go to MathiasMethod.com to learn about my Strength Journey!

The Definition Of RAW

Now let's start off with a definition of what we powerlifters consider a lift to be done "RAW".

"RAW" determines the assistance you are allowed to use for training and testing your lifts. What we consider to be RAW in this book is the same as what most sanctioned Powerlifting Competitions also consider to be RAW.

This is different than what is considered to be 100% RAW. 100% RAW means without any assistive equipment at all, as if you were only lifting in shorts and a t-shirt.

For this program we allow for some safety equipment to accommodate more people and promote safety of the lifter, above all else.

To be considered RAW you can use the assistance of:

- ☑ **a weight lifting belt,**
- ☑ **deadlift socks or shin guards,**
- ☑ **and chalk as needed.**

This amount of equipment promotes safety of the lifter while allowing for only necessary assistance. Overall, the lifter has to do the lift, not the equipment.

The more equipment you use, the more you have to rely on for max day. It is best to only use what you need to be safe and save the rest for when you absolutely need it.

Drugs and Supplements

Being RAW also does not allow the use of drugs or special supplement regiments that greatly improve a lifter's strength, recovery or muscle growth. Basically, if you would fail a drug test, then it is not RAW.

To be clear, no supplements are needed to make this program work as effectively as possible. End of story.

Lifting Equipment

Lifting equipment is anything that directly improves your ability to lift more weight. This could be very light assistive gear, such as knee or elbow sleeves, all the way up to extremely supportive gear, such as lifting suits.

One of the most common pieces of equipment to be used is a lifting belt. When used properly, a lifting belt allows you to better brace your core for stabilization by increasing the intra-abdominal pressure placed on your spine. By increasing stabilization you are enabled to lift heavier loads.

Chalk is another common lifting tool that is always permitted, as needed, to help you grip the bar, but only use it if you need it for extra support. Apply a light amount to your palms and all five fingers to take away any moisture, allowing you to grip the bar better. As the weight gets heavier you can use more.

One tool you should almost NEVER USE is lifting straps. If you need to use lifting straps, then you are going too heavy. You need to build up your grip, not cover up the issue. We will talk more on this later, but the only time you should ever use straps is if you are doing partial range of motion lifts, such as rack pulls, and using 110% of your max. Everything else, you need to be able to hold onto yourself.

Equipment can improve lifter strength and safety, but can also have adverse effects when used improperly.

If any one piece of equipment is used too frequently, then it will limit your body's ability to grow stronger in that area. Essentially, the equipment will become a crutch that then must be used every time training occurs in order to keep up with the strength developed in other non-supported areas.

The most effective way to use equipment is only when it is necessary. For example, when using light to moderate loads (<75%) avoid using any equipment at all to build greater strength in all areas. Then when you put on equipment for maximal loads (>80%) you will be that much stronger.

Even if you have an injury, only use the equipment when you need it. If your injury does not hurt, then do not cover it up with equipment. Allow it to grow stronger.

When you are building strength, use little to no equipment.

When you are testing strength, use whatever you can to improve your lift.

THE DEADLIFT

The Deadlift is one of the most brutal and beneficial lifts there is. It is brutal because you have to lift a heavy weight from a dead stop, starting in a disadvantaged position, but it is so beneficial because it improves ALL of your other lifts!

The Deadlift builds muscle mass throughout your entire body and tests your full body strength like nothing else can. Nothing can improve your hip, core, back and grip strength as much as deadlifts, and nothing can replace it.

If you have a strong deadlift, then you probably have a brutally strong body from head to toe!

It is such a simple lift, yet so hard that very few people actually do them. Not to mention that many gyms don't allow deadlifts, or have terrible set-ups for them. If that is your gym, then I highly recommend you go somewhere else that actually promotes strength and doesn't hold you back from reaching your goals.

Overall, the deadlift tests you physically and mentally with its brutality, but can make you feel super human.

No ordinary person has every deadlifted 600+ pounds. It takes hard work, dedication and an internal fire to reach that achievement, and every pound after. If you have it in you, then you have the strength to do anything you desire.

It is you versus the weight in front of you. A weight that can take you from ordinary to extraordinary. All you have to do is pick it up.

DEADLIFT EVERYDAY

You may not know it, but we deadlift every single day! Everyday we bend over and pick things up! We pick up shoes, boxes, tools, groceries, babies and more!

The problem is, so many people don't know how to deadlift properly and therefore think that deadlifts are bad for your back. Saying that deadlifts are bad for your back is the same as saying walking is bad for your feet. Deadlifts are not bad for your back. Improper deadlifts are bad, just like walking incorrectly is bad for your feet, knees and hips.

The deadlift teaches you one of the most valuable mechanical motions our body was designed to do; the Hip Hinge. The Hip Hinge is simply bending at the hips as if doing a bow, then standing. This is something we do everyday and need to learn how to improve for better posture, core strength, and to maintain a healthy back.

Regardless of what some ignorant people say, learning how to deadlift like this IS good for your back! Physical therapists even teach back patients in recovery how to deadlift properly so that they not only strengthen their back, but learn to set the weight in their hips instead of their back.

I have heard stories of grandmothers in tears after learning how to deadlift simply because they realize that now they can finally pick up their grandchildren. That is why you should teach everyone you know how to deadlift!

Teach them how to deadlift so that they learn how to brace their core properly and set the weight in their hips, which are designed to support our body as it bends over.

Now, you don't need to bring grandma to the gym and load up the weight. Instead just teach what you learn in this book to others with the things around them. You can teach how to pick up a small weight, a box, a baby or anything you have available!

That will not only keep them safe, but make them stronger too, and we all need to get stronger!

Deadlift For Beginners

How we teach the deadlift to a beginner is different than how we teach it to a more advanced lifter. This is because beginners are still figuring out their body's leverages and what works best for them while an advanced lifter knows what does and does not work for them based on experience.

When you are just starting out and discovering how your body moves when picking up weight, begin by doing what is comfortable. Stand where it is comfortable, grab the bar where it is comfortable, and get into a comfortable position to pull from. From there you can start making minor adjustments to learn proper technique and see what works best for you.

For the deadlift it is actually easier to start learning how to do the lift correctly from the top. Simply begin by picking the weight straight up however you are comfortable, so you are standing with it in your hands. From there, lower the weight slowly, under control, making sure to keep the weight tight against your legs all the way down. When the weight touches the ground, with the bar still against your shins, then you have found your proper deadlift position. Try to get set into this same position every time before you lift the weight.

Remember to always maintain control of the weight and don't let the weight control you.

If you need to change something then make small changes. Remember, small changes make a big difference, so do not do anything drastic. If you need to change your stance, hand or hip position, then do so one inch at a time.

Also, realize that things are going to take some time. Just be patient and soon enough you will be lifting like a pro!

Overall, beginners should focus on the basics and getting the general movement down before trying to apply every detail. The details will come. After deadlifting for a while you'll start to feel what works better for you versus someone else, and as your body changes, so will your technique. Focus on strength first, and improve your technique over time.

Note: *It is recommended that all beginners do conventional deadlifts,* *because it builds more full body strength and is easier to position than Sumo deadlift, in which you need to have a lot of hip mobility to get into proper position for. Learn proper Deadlift Principles with conventional deadlifts, then after you can lift at least two times your bodyweight you can start to play around with Sumo Deadlifts to see if they work better for you, but conventional is your base.*

Deadlift For Advanced Lifters

Advanced lifters are those that have been deadlifting for over a year and have developed a strong base of strength. If you have not been deadlifting for at least this long, I highly recommend you start with my *Base Of Strength Program* (see page 6) to build up all 3 of your base lifts while getting a lot of deadlift practice in.

Also, any beginners you know should start off with that program before advancing to the advanced program in this book.

An advanced lifter should be specific and focus on the details while their subconscious does the most basic aspects of the lift for them. This means taking a quick moment before every single lift to go through a checklist of specifics you need to perfect your technique.

Deadlift Checklist

As you get set and prepare to pull, take a quick moment to check:

- ☑ **Are your feet grabbing the ground?**
- ☑ **Are your knees pushed out?**
- ☑ **Are your glutes flexed?**
- ☑ **Is your core braced; front, back and sides?**
- ☑ **Are you pulling the bar into you?**
- ☑ **Are you leaning back and sticking your chest out?**
- ☑ **Are you confident and focused on your lift?**

If you can answer "Yes" to all of these questions, then you are perfectly set to lift big. The next step is to perfect your lifting technique.

The deadlift is a lift that is never perfect and needs constant tweaking. You can always move smoother. You can always drive harder. You can always brace tighter. There is always something to improve and focus on.

Not only that, but as the weight gets heavier and your body changes, so too will your leverages. For example, if you weigh 225lbs. and are lifting any weight that is 225lbs. or lighter, then you can practically just stand straight up with it, where if you are lifting 400, 500 and even 600lbs. you are going to have to lean back more each time to counterbalance the weight more so that it doesn't shoot you forward off balance.

That is one of the major difficulties of new lifters, and even advanced lifters, when they start to move past their bodyweight or even greatly increase the load, the technique changes. So make sure that you are always checking your technique for improvements.

With every workout, try to focus on one or two aspects of your technique to improve on. If you need help, asking a knowledgeable friend or trainer can really help. They can give you feedback both during your set and immediately after to help you see what needs to improve.

If you don't have that option, you can always record yourself. Just try to video from multiple angles to make sure no technique issues are hiding from the camera angle you chose.

You can also ask me anytime! You can tag me on Instagram @MathiasMethod or Facebook @MathiasMethodStrength asking for some tips and I would be happy to take a look at your lifts!

If we don't get back to you within day, then you can always message us or try my personal account @RyanJMathias. I am active on all accounts daily, but I am also a busy guy. I will get to as many as I can as often as I can, so please be patient with me if the response is not immediate.

Just remember, your deadlift is NEVER going to be perfect! There is always something to improve! If you are not improving, then you are limiting your full potential.

Now let's find what you need to improve and go deadlift!

DEADLIFT PRINCIPLES

All proper deadlift technique will have the same principles, no matter your stance or hand placement, that must be followed for safe and effective technique. These principles are presented below.

- ☑ **Hips drive forward as you stick your chest out and drive shoulders back.**

- ☑ **Bar is pulled in against your legs during the entire lift.**

- ☑ **Back flat with a neutral spine; no rounding or arching.**

- ☑ **Knees and hips extend simultaneously to lockout.**

- ☑ **Arms stay locked with shoulders back and down.**

- ☑ **Knees are pressed out to open the hips.**

- ☑ **Feet are locked into the ground.**

- ☑ **Knees stay behind the bar.**

　　　These Deadlift Principles apply to all deadlifts.

Any deadlift that follows these principles is a perfect deadlift! Speed is not important. Technique and control of the weight is.

Beyond these principles, there are two main deadlift variations that can change how your deadlift looks and is used. These are conventional, or standard, and sumo deadlifts.

CONVENTIONAL VS SUMO

When it comes to the deadlift many people have a difficulty choosing between a conventional deadlift stance or a sumo deadlift stance.

- **Conventional:** Closer stance where you grab the bar outside of your stance width.

- **Sumo:** Wider stance where you grab the bar inside of your stance width.

Both deadlifting styles are correct and simply focus on different leverages to lift the weight.

Choosing between the two simply has to do with using your leverages to your advantage. Everyone's body is different so everyone has different leverages.

Note: Regardless of your stance, the bottom 45-degrees of torso lean is hamstring dominant and the top 45-degrees is glute dominant.

CONVENTIONAL DEADLIFT

First, Conventional Deadlifts are the most basic form of deadlifts. This is where your feet are generally shoulder width or closer, and you grab the bar outside of your stance width.

This style places more stress on your hips, hamstrings and lower back, to lift the weight. Generally, shorter lifters like this style, as it benefits those with short legs and a long torso, but it can be effective for anyone that has strong glutes, hamstrings and lower back muscles.

When it comes to building strength, conventional deadlift improves sumo deadlift, but sumo deadlift does little to improve conventional deadlifts. This is because sumo is leg dominant with back and hip assistance, and has a decreased range of motion where conventional has a greater range of motion and is hip and back dominant.

You will get a lot stronger by building up your conventional deadlift, which is a brute strength lift, where sumo is a technical lift. Yes, you do still have to put the work in for sumo, but conventional is straight up physically harder where sumo is harder technique wise. You can grind through a bad conventional deadlift, where if you do sumo incorrectly, there is no way you are getting the weight up. The lift has to be perfect every time.

I recommend that all beginners do conventional deadlifts, because it builds more full body strength and is easier to position than Sumo deadlift, in which you have to have a lot of hip mobility to get into proper position for. Learn proper Deadlift Principles with conventional deadlifts, then after you can lift at least two times your bodyweight you can start to play around with Sumo Deadlifts to see if they work better for you, but conventional is your base.

SUMO DEADLIFT

Next, Sumo Deadlifts are a more advanced form of deadlifts, because they require more technique and mobility to perform correctly. Sumo deadlift is where your feet are placed wide and you grab the bar close, commonly shoulder width or so.

This style places more stress on your legs to squat the weight up, as your hips are placed in a disadvantaged position. Generally, taller lifters like this style, as it decreases the range of motion and helps them get lower.

With this style your hips are closer to the bar compared to a conventional deadlift with a more vertical torso, which takes the stress off of your lower back and places it on your legs.

This decreased back stress allows sumo deadlifters to typically handle more overall work with deadlifts, as recovery will be easier.

Another advantage is the decrease range of motion, and therefore total work done, compared to conventional deadlifts, but the start of the lift will be more difficult.

To become proficient at sumo deadlift, positioning and technique are key. If you cannot get into the proper positioning by externally rotating your hips enough, then sumo deadlift is not for you.

With conventional deadlifts, if you get out of position you can usually fight through it, where in sumo deadlifts if you get out of position, then it is almost impossible to grind through to lift the weight. Sumo deadlifts also require a lot more leg strength and hip mobility, which generally favors women, who naturally have both.

If you have already built up significant strength with conventional deadlifts, and you are able to open your hips (like the splits) well, then you may want to try Sumo Deadlifts for a while to see if they work better for you.

Both styles have their benefits, but it is up to you to decide. Overall, just choose the stance that best utilizes your leverages.

PART 2

PERFECTING YOUR TECHNIQUE

DEADLIFT TECHNIQUE GUIDE

The Ultimate Deadlift Guide

This one-of-a-kind Deadlift Guide gives you all the tools you need to deadlift more weight than ever!

- ☑ **How To Choose Your Grip**
- ☑ **Breathing and Bracing Techniques**
- ☑ **Proper Set-Up**
- ☑ **Proper Lifting Technique** (for sumo and conventional styles)
- ☑ **Technique Checklist**
- ☑ **Common Mistakes and How To Correct Them**
- ☑ **Top Accessory Exercises**
- ☑ **Deadlift Variations**
- ☑ **Tips and Tricks**

Read on to start building your strongest deadlift ever!

How To Deadlift Stronger

Choosing Your Grip

First, your grip strength is the biggest limiting factor in your overall deadlift strength. If you can't hold onto the weight, then it doesn't matter how strong the rest of your body is.

You need to be constantly improving your grip strength in order to lift more weight. The best way to do this is by simply deadlifting, without the use of lifting straps or any assistive gear. Deadlifting for reps and with more weight, both are beneficial, as long as you are holding the weight yourself. The more you practice, the stronger your grip will become.

This will actually improve all of your lifts as your hands turn into crushing machines that can more and more weight!

THERE ARE 3 DIFFERENT GRIPS YOU CAN USE WHEN DEADLIFTING:

- **Double-Overhand**

- **Hook Grip**

- **Over-Under** (pictured above)

Double-Overhand

Double-Overhand is where you grab the bar with both palms facing towards you, and thumbs wrapped around the outside. This is a very weak grip, but perfect for improving your grip strength.

All lifters should use this grip during as many warm-up sets as possible, until the weight gets too heavy to hold, in order to build up more grip strength.

Hook Grip

Hook Grip is similar to double-overhand, as your palms are facing towards you, but you hook your thumb under the bar and wrap it with your middle and pointer fingers. This is an advanced grip technique, generally used by Olympic Weightlifters and sumo deadlifters, and will cause serious pain in your thumbs until you get used to it.

The benefit of this grip is symmetry as you get to keep both hands in the same position and have your shoulders aligned, while decreasing any elbow stress your legs may cause while pulling from a sumo stance.

If you have long fingers, and do Sumo Deadlift, you may want to give this a try, but it is not necessary for any lifter.

Over-Under

Over-Under grip is the most common, and strongest, grip. This is where you place one hand palm facing in and one hand palm facing out. It does not matter which hand faces which way and you can switch it anytime.

The benefit of this grip is that it can be used without causing a lot of pain, and allows you to hold the most weight, because if the bar starts to slip out of one hand, it then rolls deeper into the other hand, and vice versa.

This is the grip most dead lifters with big numbers use and is recommended for all beginners after they can no longer keep hold of the weight with double-overhand grip.

Beyond these grips, if you still have trouble holding the weight, you can use chalk to get a better grip of the bar. Chalk takes away all the moisture from your hands, which is great when you are getting sweaty, and helps you stick to the bar better. Only use chalk when you need too though, as you build more strength without it.

However, when you do use it, cover your entire palm, four fingers and thumb with a light layer. More is not always better. Just use what you need, and when you are having a lot of grip trouble, then you can make your entire palm covered in white.

Never use straps unless you absolutely have too, and if you do, then make sure you are working on your grip strength often. Use grip strength machines, and hold all your heavy deadlifts at the top for 5+ seconds to quickly improve your strength.

Next, how you breathe during your deadlifts can greatly influence your maximal strength. What you may have been taught before is to breathe in as you descend during a lift and breathe out as you stand back up. This is good if you are in a cardio class using extremely light weights, and just need to keep your endurance up, but if you are looking to get stronger this is one of the worst things you can do.

By breathing in as you descend, your body is not as tight as it can be, and is, therefore, unstable. It is similar to deadlifting on a trampoline versus on solid ground. The more stable you are, the more you can lift. So you need to think more about how you are going to breathe during your deadlifts than what people do for general fitness.

If you want to get stronger, or build muscle, then you need to lift heavy, and to lift heavy you need to have your body braced as tightly as possible to have the most strength for your lift. For that you should use what is called the Valsalva Maneuver, which promotes the greatest amount of strength by increasing your spine stabilization through increased intra-abdominal pressure. The two versions of this breathing technique are described next.

VALSALVA MANEUVER

Suck in as much air as you can and hold it in, attempting to create as much intra-abdominal pressure as you can, to stabilize your spine. Then press your lips closed to hold the air in while flexing all of the musculature surrounding your entire torso, and forcing the air deep down into your abdomen.

Think of your torso as a soda can you are trying to fill up and pressurize. You have your pelvic floor as the base, your diaphragm as the top, and all your abdominal (front, back and side) musculature making the outer walls of the can. You want to fill the can with air and flex everything around it as tight as possible to keep the air in.

Your lifting belt can help with this, but make sure that you do not tighten it too much or you will put a dent in the can, and if you dent a can even slightly, the can crushes. Always keep your belt loose enough so that you can put 4 fingers of your hand down into the belt against your stomach with ease, while you are relaxed. Then when you brace you want to think of bracing out against the belt so that it gets filled up tightly and your fingers can no longer fit in.

The valsalva maneuver greatly increases your blood pressure and should only be held for 1-2 maximal repetitions, or when you are using over 90% of your maximum. Sets with more than 1-3 reps, or under 90% of your maximum should use the Partial Valsalva Maneuver.

PARTIAL VALSALVA MANEUVER

This is the same as the Valsalva Maneuver, except you exhale after getting past the sticking point of the lift. This helps to decrease the overall blood pressure increase created by the pressure and allows for more fluid reps to be performed, while still having a very strong lift.

For the deadlift, start to breathe out, while still bracing your core, after the weight is clearly above your knees. Then breathe in again at the top of every rep to re-brace.

BREATHE IN BEFORE YOU LIFT

For the deadlift, you need to get tight while you are standing, before you bend down to pick up the weight. If you bend over first, you have already put yourself out of position and are losing strength by the

second. Breathe in and brace at the top, then hold your breathe as you bend over to grab the bar and lift.

The longer you stay bent over before you lift, the more strength you will lose. Try to lift the weight within 3 seconds of bending over to keep the most strength built up.

Conventional Deadlift

- **Teach Hip-Hinge Mechanics**
- **Test Full Body, Hip-Hinge and Core Stabilization Strength**
- **Build Full Body, Hip-Hinge and Core Stabilization Strength**

PRIME MOVERS

- **Hamstring Complex** (Legs)
- **Glutes** (Hips)
- **Quadriceps** (Legs)

SET-UP

Your deadlift set-up is all about creating tension in the right places without wasting energy. You need to maintain that same tightness during the entire lift. If you lose tightness, then you lose strength.

SET YOUR FEET

Set your feet shoulder width or closer, to where the bar is directly over your mid-foot, and turn them out slightly (10-30 degrees).

GRAB THE GROUND

Suction cup your feet to the ground by spreading your toes as wide as you can, then grasping the floor with your entire foot. Your entire foot (heel, ball of your foot, and outer edge) should stay locked into the ground.

Then, while clenching your toes into the ground like eagle claws, create torque by externally rotate your feet, as if they were to spin in place, throughout the entire motion.

This movement should flex your entire lower body from your glutes down through your entire legs so that everything is tight, and nothing is loose or relaxed.

Maintain this external rotation torque throughout the lift.

Note: By grabbing the ground with your foot you are simply creating a strong arch in your foot, not rolling your ankle. Your feet should not move out of place or come up at all during these motions. Just create a rotational pressure to stabilize your joints, while your entire foot is locked into the ground.

Brace Your Core

Suck in as much air as you can and hold it in, attempting to create as much intra-abdominal pressure as you can, to stabilize your spine. Then press your lips closed to hold the air in while flexing all of the musculature surrounding your entire torso, and forcing the air deep down into your abdomen. This is known as the Valsalva Maneuver.

If you are wearing a lifting belt, then brace out against the belt as you do this.

BEND AT THE HIPS

While staying tight and maintaining a neutral spine, bend mainly at the hips until you can grab the bar.

GRAB THE BAR

Set your hands about 3 inches outside of your shins on either side, so that you have enough room to push your knees out and not run into your arms.

After finding your preferred width, evenly set according to the power rings, spread your fingers as wide as you can as if to engulf as much of the bar in your hand as possible.

Then grasp the bar tightly with your thumbs wrapped, trying to crush the bar in your hands to take control of the weight.

This is your control point, SO TAKE CONTROL!!! Make the weight feel small while you become invincible with your crushing grip!

Then create an external rotation torque by pointing your elbows behind you.

Note: Use a double overhand-grip as often as you can, and only switch to over-under or hook grip when the weight gets too heavy to hold otherwise.

Re-brace

While keeping your entire body tight, again suck in as much air as you can and press it down deep into your abdomen increasing the intra-abdominal pressure. Hold this tightness throughout the lift.

Get Set

Fully extend your knees to reset the tension to your hips, and then push them forward as you sit your hips back until the bar touches your shins. Use the bar as leverage to maintain balance.

Maintaining a constant external rotation torque in your feet and push your knees out hard as you do this.

While keeping a neutral spine, force your head back, with your eyes straight ahead. Imagine pulling your chin straight back, and never tilt your head up.

Maintain a neutral head position (straight spine) throughout the entire lift with eyes straight ahead.

Create Tension

Pull the bar back into your legs as you position your hips back and down, chest high and back flat. This is called "pulling the slack out of the bar."

In this position your entire body should be tight and ready to pull with the weight tight up against your shins.

Your lats should be tight, arms are straight, elbows pointed back behind you, and shoulders over or behind the bar.

Tuck Your Shoulders

Keep your shoulders back and down throughout the lift.

THE PULL

PRESS INTO THE GROUND

Simultaneously press your feet into the ground, drive your hips forward and pull your shoulders back as you extend your knees and hips together until lockout.

The entire lift should be one smooth motion.

MAINTAIN CONTROL

Stay tight as you lower the bar, with perfect form, sliding against your legs all the way down. This will build strength and improve form.

If you are doing multiple reps, pause on the ground for 1-2 seconds, without bouncing the bar or losing tightness, then pull again.

If you set-up properly your body should do most of the movement for you. All you have to do is stay tight and lift.

KEY POINTS

☑ Stay tight throughout the entire set-up and lift.

☑ Grab the ground with your feet.

☑ Pull the bar into you.

☑ Torque your knees out throughout the full range of motion.

☑ Drive your feet into the ground and hips forward.

☑ Maintain a neutral spine and head position.

SUMO DEADLIFT

- **Teach Hip-Hinge Mechanics**
- **Test Full Body, Hip-Hinge and Core Stabilization Strength**
- **Build Full Body, Hip-Hinge and Core Stabilization Strength**

- **Quadriceps** (Legs)
- **Hamstring Complex** (Legs)
- **Glutes** (Hips)

The Sumo Deadlift is a variation that emphasizes more on the use of your legs squat the weight up rather than your hips and back.

With this style your hips are closer to the bar compared to a conventional deadlift with a more vertical torso, which takes the stress off of your lower back and places it on your legs.

This decreased back stress allows sumo dead lifters to typically handle more overall work with deadlifts, as recovery will be easier.

Another advantage is the decrease range of motion, and therefore total work done, compared to conventional deadlifts, but the start of the lift will be more difficult.

To become proficient at sumo deadlift, positioning and technique are key. If you cannot get into the proper positioning by externally rotating your hips enough, then sumo deadlift is not for you.

SET-UP

Your deadlift set-up is all about creating tension in the right places without wasting energy. You need to maintain that same tightness during the entire lift. If you lose tightness, then you lose strength.

SET YOUR FEET

Set your feet close enough so that your shins are nearly touching the bar outside of where your hands will be placed, and turn them out as much as you need to get your knees behind the bar when you squat down (10-45 degrees).

Find the best position for you, and if you have hip mobility problems you should try to improve them before every training session. You can do this with my *How To Warm-Up Properly For Strength Training Guide* (See page 6).

GRAB THE GROUND

Suction cup your feet to the ground by spreading your toes as wide as you can, then grasping the floor with your entire foot. Your entire foot (heel, ball of your foot, and outer edge) should stay locked into the ground.

Then, while clenching your toes into the ground like eagle claws, create torque by externally rotate your feet, as if they were to spin in place, throughout the entire motion.

This movement should flex your entire lower body from your glutes down through your entire legs so that everything is tight, and nothing is loose or relaxed.

Maintain this external rotation torque throughout the lift.

Note: By grabbing the ground with your foot you are simply creating a strong arch in your foot, not rolling your ankle. Your feet should not move out of place or come up at all during these motions. Just create a rotational pressure to stabilize your joints, while your entire foot is locked into the ground.

BRACE YOUR CORE

Suck in as much air as you can and hold it in, attempting to create as much intra-abdominal pressure as you can, to stabilize your spine.

Then press your lips closed to hold the air in while flexing all of the musculature surrounding your entire torso, and forcing the air deep down into your abdomen. This is known as the Valsalva Maneuver.

If you are wearing a lifting belt, then brace out against the belt as you do this.

BEND AT THE HIPS

While staying tight and maintaining a neutral spine, bend mainly at the hips until you can grab the bar.

GRAB THE BAR

Place your hands directly under your shoulders and hips, so that your arms are vertical, not angled in or out.

After finding your preferred width, evenly set according to the power rings, spread your fingers as wide as you can as if to engulf as much of the bar in your hand as possible.

Then grasp the bar tightly with your thumbs wrapped, trying to crush the bar in your hands to take control of the weight.

This is your control point, SO TAKE CONTROL!!! Make the weight feel small while you become invincible with your crushing grip!

Then create an external rotation torque by pointing your elbows behind you.

Note: Use a double overhand-grip as often as you can, and only switch to over-under or hook grip when the weight gets too heavy to hold otherwise.

Re-brace

While keeping your entire body tight, again suck in as much air as you can and press it down deep into your abdomen increasing the intra-abdominal pressure. Hold this tightness throughout the lift.

Get Set

Fully extend your knees to reset the tension to your hips, and then push your knees out hard as you drive your hips forward into the bar. Your hips should be down and knees behind the bar.

Use the bar as leverage to maintain balance as you get into position and keep a constant external rotation torque in your feet.

While keeping a neutral spine, force your head back, with your eyes straight ahead. Imagine pulling your chin straight back, and never tilt your head up.

Maintain a neutral head position (straight spine) throughout the entire lift with eyes straight ahead.

Create Tension

Pull the bar back into your legs as your position your hips back and down, chest high and back flat. This is called "pulling the slack out of the bar."

In this position your entire body should be tight and ready to pull with the weight tight up against your shins.

Your lats should be tight, arms are straight, elbows pointed back behind you, and shoulders over or behind the bar.

Tuck Your Shoulders

Keep your shoulders back and down throughout the lift.

THE PULL

PRESS INTO THE GROUND

Simultaneously press your feet down and out into the ground, as you drive your hips forward and pull your shoulders back, extending your knees and hips together until lockout.

The entire lift should be one smooth motion.

MAINTAIN CONTROL

Stay tight as you lower the bar, with perfect form, sliding against your legs all the way down. This will build strength and improve form.

If you are doing multiple reps, pause on the ground for 1-2 seconds, without bouncing the bar or losing tightness, then pull again.

If you set-up properly your body should do most of the movement for you. All you have to do is stay tight and lift.

KEY POINTS

- ☑ Stay tight throughout the entire set-up and lift.

- ☑ Grab the ground with your feet.

- ☑ Pull the bar into you.

- ☑ Torque your knees out throughout the full range of motion.

- ☑ Drive your feet into the ground and hips forward.

- ☑ Maintain a neutral spine and head position.

Common Deadlift Mistakes

Improper set-up

Make sure that everything is perfect before you start. If you set-up wrong, then your entire lift is going to be wrong.

You can't correct your position while lifting so you have to make it perfect before you even start to pull.

When you set-up, make sure to take your time. Don't rush it too much. You do need to be pretty quick with your deadlift set-up so that you do not lose strength by sitting in the bottom position for too long getting set, but don't rush so much that you forget something.

Even if you have to do your entire set-up multiple times, it is best to take that few extra seconds to get yourself in the best position to lift from, then rush it and risk missing a lift or getting injured.

Your set-up should be exactly the same every single time so that you are always lifting from the same perfect position and not just lazily going through the motions. If you want to lift big weight, then you need to take the time to perfect everything, including your set-up.

Losing tightness at the bottom of the deadlift

The longer you sit in the bottom position of the deadlift getting set-up, the more strength you lose. You need to get tight before you even bend over to grab the bar, and when you do, try to lift the bar within 3 seconds.

That should be long enough to set your hands and sit back into position for your pull. It may take some time to get set that quickly, but remember, most of your tightness is created before you even grab the bar.

So don't take your time at the bottom to get set up. Set-up at the top and get out of the bottom as soon as you can! The faster you can get set creating tension, the more explosive power you will save.

Also, don't rip it off the floor before you are tight. If you rip it you get forced out of position. Pull the slack out of the bar to create tension, then explode up.

Whether you are doing a conventional or a sumo deadlift where you place your hands matters, because it effects how well you can transfer energy from you into the bar.

With either style, your hands should be placed as close to directly under your shoulders as you can without getting in the way of your legs.

For sumo deadlifts this is easy, because you just let your arms hang and grab the bar where they fall. As long as your stance is wide enough that your arms are not running into your knees, then your hands are in the right place. If not, then you need to either bring your grip in or open your knees more.

For conventional deadlifts it is more common to have your arms get in the way of your legs, because your feet are generally shoulder width, and as you get set you have to drive your knees out even wider in order to get closer to the bar for more leverage. So you will need to place your hands not only outside of shoulder width, but also far enough out that your knees have all the room that they need to perform the lift correctly.

Though it seems that you should set your hands just outside of your shins to grab the bar, this prevents your knees from getting in the proper position to lift with the most power. If you grab too close, then your knees will either cave in, your arms will have to bend, or you will push the bar farther away from your center of gravity by shoving your knees forward and not out.

It is more important to have the bar as close to your hips as possible, than it is to decrease the range of motion by a few millimeters, so place pressing your knees out over grabbing the bar super close or too wide.

TURNING TOES OUT TOO MUCH

This is a common mistake for many Sumo Stance Lifters that are taught they get more power by having their toes turned out when lifting. It is true that turning your toes out helps to engage the glutes better when you lift, however, many people take it too far.

If you turn your toes out more than 45 degrees you actually decrease the amount of power you can get from your glutes by shortening the muscle too much. Muscle's are strongest in their mid-range of motion and lose power near full extension and full contraction.

For the glutes you will get the most power by turning your toes out only 10-45 degrees depending upon your stance and mobility.

Generally, with deadlifts, the wider your stance, the farther you should turn your toes out. This will help to open your hips more, as is needed for a wider stance. If you have tight hips, then you should try to improve your mobility with some of my mobility exercises on MathiasMethod.com.

TILTING YOUR HEAD BACK

Your body follows your head, meaning that if you arch your head back, then your entire spine naturally arches with it, and if you tuck your head forward, then your entire spine rounds forward. That is why head position is so important during all of your lifts, especially the deadlift.

To put your back in the strongest position, it needs to be neutral, or flat. Not arched or rounded. Arching and rounding puts a lot of unnecessary strain on your spinal column and leads to back problems that you do not want. However, if you keep a flat back, or as flat as you can make it, during your lifts, then your back will be totally safe from harm.

This all starts with your head position. You should try to keep your eyes focused on the ground about 10 feet in front of you as you lift and drive your head back, as if pulling your chin back towards your neck.

ROUNDING YOUR BACK

We have all seen those videos of people trying to pick up a weight that they have no business handling, and they do so with horrid form. Lifting weight with a rounded back is one of the worst things you can do, and greatly increases your risk of injury. Unfortunately, it is more common than not, among those that do not know how to brace properly. Hence why I am writing this book.

Back rounding occurs when you are not properly braced before your deadlift. There are a few reasons for this, but the most common is an improper set-up. If you set-up as you are supposed too, then all you have to do is maintain that same tightness during the entire lift and there should be little to no back rounding.

If you are a beginner, your back is going to be rounded. That's just the way it is. Your body is still learning how to find tension and brace properly, so it is not a big deal as long as you are keeping the weight moderate and constantly trying to maintain a flat back. As you get stronger, it will get easier.

Also, if you wear your lifting belt too tight, you will not be able to brace properly and this will lead to rounding over the belt. You should always wear your belt to where you can place your four fingers in the belt at your stomach when relaxed so that you can then brace out against the belt when you lift. If you rely on the belt to do all the work, then you are just asking to hurt yourself.

Taller lifters, and those with tight hamstrings, may also have some lower back rounding towards the bottom of the deadlift, but this is just because of mechanics and is not a big deal unless it is starting to cause pain. The only way to fix this is by simply improving the mobility of your hamstrings, but this still may not fix the issue as muscles can only go so far no matter how much you work on them. Just make sure you brace tight, and you should be fine.

BOUNCING THE WEIGHT OFF THE GROUND

Bouncing the weight off the ground during a deadlift set is the same as bouncing the weight off your chest during bench press. It is NEVER correct or okay.

DO NOT BOUNCE THE BAR OFF THE GROUND! We are here to build strength, not fake it! If you can't control the entire range, then you shouldn't lift that weight!

You should always be in control of the weight and do a short pause on the floor, while staying tight, before pulling again. That is how you build up strength at the bottom of the lift for a brutally strong deadlift like the pros!

Even doing a slight touch-and-go is okay, as long as you do not let the entire load to bounce on the ground. This causes you to lose tightness and ruins all of your other reps.

Not to mention, bouncing the weight will make you very weak for the initial pull of the deadlift, which is the hardest part on the first rep. So if you want a big deadlift, you need to work the entire range of motion to make it strong.

If you are not used to pausing on the ground it will seem very difficult at first, but after a few weeks of practice you will absolutely feel the benefits.

Knees cave in as you lift

Knees caving in is more common for Sumo stance lifters, but can happen in both styles.

If your knees are caving during conventional deadlifts, then your glutes are weak and your quads are overpowering the movement. Work on your glute strength with top end deadlifts, or rack pulls, and make sure to force your knees out hard during all your lifts.

For sumo stance lifters, the knee caves in for both those with weak glutes and those with tight hip adductors (inner thigh muscles). To correct this, simply work on mobilizing your inner thighs and hamstrings before every workout. Try to open your hips like you are doing the splits often to get your body used to it both with and without weight in your hands.

This will improve your position and make for a much stronger sumo deadlift.

It's all in the hips

The deadlift is a Hip Hinge movement, meaning that the main thing that needs to occur is bending over at the hip and cranking yourself back up. This is the same as if you were doing a bow, however, when we deadlift, we also put our legs into it.

Your back should not do any of the movement. It is simply a stabilizer that allows you to lift the weight with a neutral spine.

Though this is all true, many people are afraid of putting any stress on their back for fear of injury. Instead they attempt to squat the weight up in an awkward position that can cause even more damage.

When you deadlift YOU NEED TO USE YOUR HIPS! It is a Hip Hinge! Not a back crack or knee cave!

Put your hips into it! The Hip Hinge is one of the strongest motions the human body was designed to do and needs to be utilized properly through proper deadlift technique.

Simply set the weight into your hips when you set-up and then drive them forward to lift the weight with your legs assisting and back simply stabilizing the hinge. Anything else is incorrect.

TOP ACCESSORY EXERCISES

The best lift to build up your deadlift is the deadlift. That is the same for any lift. However, you can only deadlift so much and so often before you start overdoing it to where the benefits plateau. That is where accessory exercises come into play.

Accessory exercises allow you to get in more training volume and help to build up specific muscle groups that may need more direct attention.

For example, you can use goodmornings to build up hip strength or glute-ham raises to build up hamstring strength.

THESE ARE THE BEST ACCESSORY EXERCISES TO INCREASE YOUR DEADLIFT:

- **Deadlift Variations** for different stimulus.
- **Squats** for leg, hip, hamstring and core strength.
- **Glute-Ham Raises** for hamstring strength.
- **Weighted Planks** for core strength.
- **Good Mornings** for hip and core strength.
- **Pull-ups** and **Barbell Rows** for back strength.
- **Plyometric Jumps** for maximal strength and explosive power.

There are thousands of other exercises that can help build up your strength for deadlifts, but these are the most effective ones that have a direct carry-over to your deadlift strength. Improve these, and your deadlift strength will absolutely go up.

These are also the accessory exercises you will be doing in any of of our Mathias Method Strength Programs, including the 12-Week Deadlift Program in this book!

These exercises are hard, but they are also highly effective in building full body strength like nothing else can. Work these often and your strength will shoot up!

Deadlift Variations

Lift variations allow for a different stimulus and can allow for new growth, building up specific parts of the lift. This is also a great way to target specific muscle groups that may be lagging behind and need more attention.

Variation can be simple or complex, but to build strength towards the main movements, it is important not to vary too far from the original lift. Start with simple variations before moving into more complex changes.

It doesn't make sense to vary the range of motion so drastically to where it is a completely different lift that may not have any carryover to your actual deadlift. For deficits, you really only need a 1 inch deficit. For rack pulls, your starting position should always be below your shin.

Here are some Common Variations you can use to spice up your lifts:

- **Stance or Grip Width**

- **Deficit Deadlifts**

- **Pauses above or below the knee**

- **Rack or Block Pulls**

- **Accommodating Resistance (Bands or Chains)**

- **Assistive Gear**

Variation is a great way to spice up your training, but needs to be limited. If you truly want to build a lot of strength, then you need to put in the work and not just find ways to make lifts easier.

Variation is best used with advanced lifters who have already mastered their lifting technique and progress is stalling. Beginners should rarely use variations in the main lifts if at all, because the best variation to build up your deadlift is just doing more deadlifts. It is only after standard deadlifts are not working well that you should try something different. Intermediate lifters can try some variations infrequently, but most of the work should focus on perfecting the main lift.

PART 3

BUILDING STRENGTH

12-WEEK DEADLIFT PROGRAM

Maximize Your Deadlift Strength!

This program is based on the Mathias Method Strength System.

12-weeks. 12-weeks of hard work. That is all it takes.

During that time you will be significantly improving your deadlift technique and building an incredible amount of strength. Both of which will have you more than ready to set a brand new PR!

However, it won't be easy. Over the next 12-weeks you will be taken on a journey that will lead you to something you have never done before. You will be pushed and tested every step of the way. You will learn new ways of building strength that you may have never learned otherwise and you will take your strength beyond what you may have ever imagined. When you are done, you will be changed and look back at where you used to be only to see how far you have come.

The only thing to do next is ask, "what's next?"! The answer, is up to you…

Note: This is a 12-week cyclical program that is meant to be done over-and-over again for as long as you wish. After completing a cycle, you can immediately start back over at week 1. However, I recommend you take 1-2 weeks between cycles to just go into the gym and have some fun doing workouts with less strict programming. This will give you a mental break from the strict programming and help you come back refreshed and ready for the next 12-weeks.

This Deadlift Program does not promise that you will achieve a 600+ lb deadlift in just 12-weeks. But I do guarantee that, if you put in the work, your strength will go up over-and-over again until you reach your full deadlifting potential! Whether that is 600+lbs or not is up to you!

PROGRAM DETAILS

This is a 12-Week Strength Program that focuses on increasing your deadlift max. In it I will guide you through the exact work you need to do in order to reach your new Deadlift Max, and eventually to Deadlift 600+ lbs.!

This program can be used to repeatedly improve your deadlift until you reach your goal of deadlifting 400, 500 and even 600+ pounds! After you finish one 12 week phase, simply take a week off from deadlifting and then begin again!

For many, this program may seem like a lot, but to deadlift more than before you have to put in more work than before. You have to do hard things, because hard things make you stronger.

This program is best for lifters with at least a year of deadlift experience under their belt. If you have not been practicing your deadlifts for that long or more, then you will benefit more from my *Base Of Strength Training Program* (see page 6), which is made to help you improve your squat, bench press and deadlift, simultaneously.

THIS PROGRAM HAS 3 PHASES:

1. **Volume Phase**

2. **Strength Phase**

3. **Max Phase**

Each Phase is 3 weeks long with every 4th week being a deload before starting the next phase.

Phase 1 - Volume

The first 3 weeks of your training is the Volume Phase. This Phase will focus on increasing your total work capacity with light to moderate weight and a lot of volume.

This is the time to improve your technique and reset your deadlift so that your body is ready for the more intense work ahead without becoming over fatigued.

This Volume Work is also used as a "Strength Reset" in which you give your body time off from maximal work to prepare it for more progress at your new found strength. This Phase is vital for your maximal strength, and will have your body craving more intense weights when complete.

Deload Weeks

Every 4th week in this program is a deload and recovery week. This week allows your body to catch up on recovery, build up other weak areas and prepare you for the high intensity workouts the following week.

This is the time to focus on other accessory lifts, that will help to build up your body's weak areas and improve your overall strength.

Squats will be your Main Lift for these weeks and you will not do any deadlifts during your Strength Workout. This will give your back a short break and help you prepare for the intense workouts ahead.

Week 8 is another deload week, and is vital to allow your body enough time to recover fully before taking on your most intense workouts during your 4 week Peaking Phase!

Phase 2 - Strength

The next 3 weeks (5-7) are your Strength Phase. These workouts combine intensity and volume to build up the greatest amount of strength.

These workouts will be long and hard, but you will feel like a true Strength Warrior if you can get through them without being crushed by the weight!

Take your time with every set and make sure that you are moving with a purpose on every rep. Be in control of the weight, and do not let the weight take control of you.

PHASE 3 - MAX

The final 4 weeks, including your deload week, are what is called your Max Phase, or Peaking Phase. These workouts are designed to increase your maximal strength and prepare you to crush your peak week!

This is where you have your most intense workouts before backing off for at least 10-14 days in order to hit a Strength Peak where your body is ready to lift the most weight for your main lift.

These 4 weeks are crucial to nail perfectly in order to peak at the right time and get the greatest improvement in your deadlift max.

Make sure your recovery is on point and you do not do anything out of the ordinary during these 4 weeks.

PEAK WEEK

Peak Week starts with your Week 11 - Workout 1 and goes until your Max Day.

You will start Week 11 by working up to the heaviest weight that you feel you can do 2-3 clean reps with. This should be at least 90% of your old maximum, but can also be well over your previous 100% max, depending on how well the program has worked for you so far. This is going to be your heaviest workout of the cycle, but it is not meant for you to do an all time max. This is still a preparation for your max day, so save some.

When you find your perfect weight, you are going to do 5-10 singles with it, stopping when form begins to break down too much. If form breaks down before you reach 5 reps then you need to significantly drop the weight to where you can do clean singles. If you are working into a competition, then this working weight should be your opening lift.

This workout should give you a good idea of what your max should be on max day. If this workout goes well, then you can expect to hit 110% of this weight on max day. For example, if you were able to do 5-10 good singles with 450 lbs. then you can expect to deadlift 500+ lbs. on max day.

This is your last maximal workout before your max day and you should plan to max 10-14 days after this workout.

You will finish Week 11 off with your normal Base Work before moving to week 12.

Week 12 is also a deload week in which you will do minimal work and very low intensity for all of your lifts, so that your body is more than ready for Max Day.

You will start the week by doing only 8 singles at 50% of your deadlift max followed by 5 sets of only 3 reps for squats, then your normal Accessory Work. Keep your accessory work light and easy on this day and just get some movement in. You do not want to take the week off from lifting, but you also do not want to fatigue yourself with any of your workouts.

Keep all your workouts light and easy this week and have at least 1-3 days off from all training before max day.

MAX DAY

Max Day is your day. It is the day you have prepared for with every workout over the past 12 weeks. You are ready for this and you should wake up feeling super human!

Make sure that you are fully rested on the days leading up to your Max Day and your nutrition is on point. Stay hydrated and eat normally.

Do not try any new supplements or food protocols around this day. You don't need to be overly stuffed or caffeinated to lift heavy. You have been preparing for weeks and you are ready. Just go do it.

Take your time on Max Day. Take your time waking up. Take your time eating before hand. Take your time getting to the gym and take your time warming up. This is your day so let it last.

Warm-up slowly and take as long as you need between sets. As you get over 80% your rest should be between 5-10 minutes, not more or less.

Make sure everything is feeling good and move violently. If the weight is light, then it should look light. Drive into every rep as if it is your max and make sure your body is prepared to be explosive with that new max.

If you prepared properly, then this day will be easy for you.

When you are ready, go for it! Be confident in yourself and show the world WHO YOU ARE!!! It's Game Time! Go dominate!

Remember to tag @MathiasMethod when you post your new PR so I can see how you did!

If you want some good Game Day Motivation, then check out my motivation book *Motivated Mindset* (see page 6)! It will get you fired up for anything you pursue in your life no matter the challenges you face!

HOW TO MAX OUT PROPERLY

How you work up to your max can greatly effect your maximal strength. The goal is to stimulate your body for a maximal lift without over-fatiguing yourself to where you have major strength loss.

If you go in and do a bunch of unnecessary reps you are just going to be waisting energy. It is better to do more sets and less reps to conserve energy than try to do a full workout before hand. You wouldn't run a mile to warm up for a sprint, so don't make the same mistake here. All you need to do is feel the weight. When the weight feels good, move up.

Below we give you a common max out protocol, but you can add more sets if needed. Remember, the goal is to get your body prepared for maximal weight, and not fatigue you.

Take your time between sets and go when you are ready keeping the reps low. Remember to be explosive with every single rep as if it is a maximal lift.

- **Bar x 5-10**

- **30-40% x 5-10**

- **50-60% x 3-5**

- **70-75% x 3**

- **80-85% x 1-3**

- **90-95% x 1**

- **100-105% x 1**

- **105%+ x 1**

Add multiple sets as needed.

All percentages are based on your projected max calculated by your Week 11 - Workout 1 working weight multiplied by 110%. If you used 545 lbs. as your working weight for all 5-10 singles, then your projected max is 600 lbs.

If you had to lower the weight for that workout, then use the lower weight to calculate your projected max.

It is better to warm-up a little lighter than it is to warm-up going too heavy.

Weekly Workout Schedule

This deadlift program has you deadlifting 2 times per week. Workout 1 is your Strength Work in which you will be improving your deadlift's maximal strength through intense training. Workout 2 is your Base Work in which you will be practicing your technique and increasing your overall training volume.

Your first workout of the week should focus on the lift you want to improve. In this case, that is your deadlift. Make sure that you have at least 1 rest day before this training day, in which you do no gym or cardio work. That will allow you to be the most fresh and prepared to take on the challenging workout ahead.

The second deadlift workout of the week should occur 3-4 days after your first deadlift workout. It would also be best to have a recovery day before this training day, but it is not required. Just make sure that you are recovering enough.

All other workouts throughout the week should not include deadlifts or squats of any kind. Avoid fatiguing your legs and back on other training days, but you can use any training split you want.

This is the training split we have found most effective for this training program.

Day 1 - **Deadlift Workout 1** (Strength Work)

Day 2 - Off

Day 3 - Bench Press Workout 1

Day 4 - Off

Day 5 - **Deadlift Workout 2** (Base Work)

Day 6 - Bench Press Workout 2

Day 7 - Off

On all of your other training days, make sure that you do not push yourself too hard. If improving your deadlift is your main focus, then save most of your energy for your deadlift days. Just get the work in that you need for other lifts and muscle groups to stay strong. Doing a 5x5 workout at about 70% with small 5lb. jumps every week should be enough to keep your other main lifts moving forward without over stressing your body. Or get my Bench BIG Program (see page 6) to pair with this one!

#MathiasMethod   #Deadlift600

Follow @MathiasMethod on Social Media

and tag us in your #Deadlift600 workout clips!

Also, feel free to reach out anytime with your questions

or technique checks!

Deadlift Workouts

Strength Work

The first workout of each week is your "Strength Work" in which you will focus on building maximal strength. This workout will have the heaviest lifts of the training week and require the most preparation and recovery.

Over the 12 weeks the intensity will vary to allow for optimal recovery between high intensity training sessions.

The first 3 weeks will have a gradual progression as you increase your work capacity and prepare for the high demanding work load ahead. Then every 4th week is a deload week in which you will take a break from the intense lifting and work on other accessory lifts. You will not do any deadlifting for these workouts on deload weeks to allow for more recovery.

The following weeks the intensity will vary between high and moderate each week as you gradually increase your total work load up until peak week.

Peak week is the last 10-14 days before your maximal lift attempt, starting with your first workout of week 11. It is crucial that you do this properly to get maximum results.

For your Maximal Work on week 11 you will work up to the heaviest weight you feel that you can do for about 2-3 reps, but make sure that you only do 1 rep. This should be at least 90%, but can also be well over your previous 100% max, depending on how well the program has worked for you so far. You are going to do 5-10 perfect singles with this weight, stopping only when you cannot perform the squat with reasonable form. Be careful not to push yourself too hard in this workout. You want to work hard, but not get injured before max day.

After doing 5 or more singles with this weight, you can add a little weight, but no more than 3-5% if you feel good. If it is getting heavy during your first 5 singles, then maintain the same weight until form breaks down.

Week 12 is your official peak week in which you use very light weight and just work the movement. You want to stretch out the movement and allow for blood flow, but focus on recovery above all else.

Then, 4-7 days later test out your max by gradually working up in weight. Make sure that you get plenty of rest this week and only max out on a day that you feel ready, and not fatigued. Your other workouts during this week should also be light and easy.

Base Work

The second workout of each week is your Base Work. This is a light to moderately intense workout to help you get in more work while improving your technique.

For your Base Work you will be doing 5 sets of 5 reps on squats before deadlifting. Most of the time you will be given a 5% range to work in. For this, work up to a weight within the range that feels good and moves well.

How you feel during these workouts will vary every week, so do not worry so much about the weight, even if you have to go lighter than expected. It is more important to focus on moving well and with perfect technique. Save the heavy stuff for your Strength Work days. Think of it as a movement and recovery workout.

As for your technique, since the weights are lighter for these workouts, every rep should be explosive and done with perfect form. Do not take it easy just because it is light. If it is light, then you should make it look easy by driving the weight up hard with every rep.

After squats you will do some light deadlifts. This is the time where you can do a variation of your deadlift and work on a weak area.

If you normally do sumo deadlifts, then your Base Work variations should all be done with a conventional stance to build up more hip and back strength. If you normally do conventional deadlifts, then consider doing 1-2 inch deficit deadlifts during these workouts to help build more strength off the floor.

Also, for these workouts, only use equipment (belt, sleeves, wraps, etc.) if needed. Try to do every set 100% RAW, if you can. This will help increase your RAW strength and make you that much stronger when you do use equipment on other days.

Week 12 you will not have any Base Work as you prepare for Max Day. Use this as a recovery day.

PROGRAM CHART

WEEK	MAIN LIFTS	SETS	REPS	% MAX
WORKOUT 1 - STRENGTH WORK				
1	Deadlift	5	5	70%
1	Squat Variation	4	8	40-45%
2	Deadlift	5	5	73%
2	Squat Variation	4	8	40-45%
3	Deadlift	5	5	75%
3	Squat Variation	4	8	40-45%
4	Squat	6	4	75%
5	Deadlift	8	3	80%
5	Squat Variation	4	6	50-55%
6	Deadlift	6	4	77%
6	Squat Variation	4	6	50-55%
7	Deadlift	6	2	85%
7	Squat Variation	4	6	50-55%
8	Squat	6	3	80%
9	Deadlift	5	2	87%
9	Squat Variation	4	5	55-60%
10	Deadlift	6	3	80%
10	Squat Variation	4	5	55-60%
11	*Deadlift	5-10	1	*90% +
11	Squat Variation	4	5	55-60%
12	Deadlift	8	1	50%
12	Squat	5	3	50%

WEEK	MAIN LIFTS	SETS	REPS	% MAX
WORKOUT 2 - BASE WORK				
1	Squat	5	5	50%
1	Deadlift Variation	4	8	50-55%
2	Squat	5	5	55%
2	Deadlift Variation	4	8	50-55%
3	Squat	5	5	60%
3	Deadlift Variation	4	8	50-55%
4	Squat	5	5	65%
4	Deadlift Variation	4	6	55-60%
5	Squat	5	5	65-70%
5	Deadlift Variation	4	6	55-60%
6	Squat	5	5	65-70%
6	Deadlift Variation	4	6	55-60%
7	Squat	5	5	65-70%
7	Deadlift Variation	4	5	60-65%
8	Squat	5	5	70-75%
8	Deadlift Variation	4	5	60-65%
9	Squat	5	5	70-75%
9	Deadlift Variation	4	5	60-65%
10	Squat	5	5	70-75%
10	Deadlift	5	3	65%
11	Squat	5	5	65-70%
11	Deadlift	8	1	60%
12	**Deadlift**	*Max Day*		

*Week 11 - DO NOT MAX! Use the heaviest weight you can do 2-3 reps with for all 5-10 sets.

- **Weeks 1-4, 6, 8 and 10 (Workout 1) -** AMRAP the last set of deadlifts using the same working weight. AMRAP = As Many Reps As Possible *(always leave 1-2 reps in the tank)*.

- **Weeks 5, 7 and 9 (Workout 1) -** Work up to a Daily Max of 1-3 reps after all your deadlift sets are complete. Work up slowly taking as many sets as needed, but do not reach failure. Just move something heavy. If the weights did not move well during your sets, then just do an AMRAP for your last set with your working weight instead.

- **DO NOT change your weights after achieving a new max during the program** - Depending on your experience level, you may very well surpass your old max when doing your daily maxes. This is expected and accounted for in the programming. Do not change anything.

- **Week 11 -** DO NOT MAX OUT! Read the "Peak Week" section for details.

- **Always AMRAP the last set of squats on Base Work days.**

All percentages are based on your current max before beginning the program, not your projected max at the end.

Base your squat max on your belt-less squat max, as most if not all of your squats will be done without a belt to help build up your core.

If you do not know your max, then do a low estimate. As in, something you know you can do 2-3 good reps with at the start of the program. You will actually get more out of the program if you go a little lighter than you need too versus going a bit too heavy.

Warm-Up:

The Daily 30	1-3 Rounds
Weighted Pull-Ups	- x 25 total
Box Jumps (optional)	3-5 x 3

Technique Work:

Deadlift (<50%)	3 x 5

Main Lifts:

Deadlift	See Program Chart
*Overload Set	See Program Chart Notes
Squat Variation	See Program Chart

Accessory Work:

Glute-Ham Raises / Leg Curls	5-10 x 6-10
Dumbbell Rows	5 x 6-8
Hammer Curls	4 x 8-10
Side Planks	3 x 45 sec.
Mobility Work	10+ min.

*Done after your main work is complete, and never to failure.

Go to MathiasMethod.com for in-depth exercise descriptions.

WORKOUT 2 - BASE WORK

Warm-Up:

The Daily 30	1-3 Rounds
Pull-Ups	- x 30-50

Technique Work:

Deadlift (<50%)	3 x 5

Main Lifts:

Squat	See Program Chart
Deadlift Variation	See Program Chart

Accessory Work:

Leg Press	5 x 10-15
Lat Pull-Downs	5 x 10-15
Dumbbell Curls	3 x 10-15
Weighted Planks	3 x 30-60 sec.
Mobility Work	10+ min.

Go to MathiasMethod.com for in-depth exercise descriptions.

WORKOUT DETAILS

All workouts and training protocols follow the Mathias Method Strength System Principles.

In the Mathias Method Strength System we don't train muscle groups. We train movements and base our workouts on improving one lift. This is because lifts like the squat, bench press, and deadlift are all full body lifts. They take your entire body working in unison to perfect and do not target one specific area.

By building up these powerful compound movements we will develop strength and muscle throughout our entire body.

We also believe in using only the most effective accessory exercises. Big bang exercises that build big muscle and big strength. Yeah, they are hard ones and they make you brutally strong too.

This training style may be different than what you are used to, but it is what has worked for me and countless others with the same goal of getting brutally strong.

The details of your training are discussed below.

THE WARM-UP

Warm-ups are just what you think. They are simply meant too, warm-up your body for the intense work ahead, not overly fatigue you.

If you are not used to doing some warm-up exercises before your main work, then it will be fatiguing at first until your body gets more conditioned. This is part of developing the work capacity to lift heavy weight, so do not skip this just because you do not feel like it. If you want to get stronger, you're gonna have to put in the work no matter how you "feel".

Warm-ups should be relatively easy and never done to failure.

Every workout you do should start with 1-3 rounds of *The Daily 30* (see page 6) to practice your movement patterns and improve mobility while you warm-up. This may seem unnecessary, but it will do wonders for your strength and help to alleviate any muscle or joint pain you have.

For both training days you will also warm-up with pull-ups. Back strength is actually one of the most important factors in providing strength for all of your lifts, which is why we have you start every workout with pull-ups to develop back strength.

If you can't do pull ups then you can use a band for assistance or replace these with heavy lat pull-downs, but if you've been training for a while you know that there really is no replacement for pull-ups. They are a vital exercise that our bodies were designed to do and need to be practiced often. They decompress your spine and build back strength like nothing else can!

Do as many sets as it takes to get to the set number of reps, never going to failure.

For weighted pull-ups you want to aim for a weight that allows you to do 5 sets of 5 reps or so. Adjust the weight as needed.

If you cannot do 10 pull-ups in a row, then either do heavy lat pull-downs for 5x10 on your Base Work training days or cut the reps down to 30 total for those workouts.

As part of your warm up on Strength Work days you can also include plyometrics. This is optional, but highly recommended.

Plyometrics have an incredible ability to prepare your body for maximal lifts through the reflexive contraction that they provide, very similar to a maximal deadlift. The key is to jump to a difficult height onto a box, but not so high that you risk missing the box. Then slowly over time try to increase the height. As the box height raises, so too will your deadlift max!

For added strength and performance, follow my How To Warm-Up Guide (see page 6) before every workout!

TECHNIQUE WORK

Exercise Technique is a crucial part of any movement based training program. Without proper technique your body will learn improper movement patterns that can hold back your strength and cause injury.

Technique is so important that it should be checked and improved every time you start a training session!

Your technique work is still part of your warm-up and therefore only light weights (<50% of your maximum) should be used to prevent over fatiguing yourself. The focus is on improving your movement pattern by utilizing perfect form, under controlled movements.

The main goals of this exercise is to prepare your body for the more intense work ahead, build up weaknesses and increase work capacity.

You should do only 3 sets of 5 perfect reps. Again, the goals are to improve the motion of this exercise and better prepare your body for the work ahead, not to pre-fatigue those muscles.

After completing your Technique Work, you are ready to begin your workout!

Start with your first exercise by doing the same number of repetitions you plan to train with for that day. If you are doing 3 reps for your working sets, do all your warm-ups with 3 reps. Start with a low intensity and work your way up slowly.

THE MAIN LIFT

The main lift, or main lifts, of any given workout, is the focus point of the session, where you put in the most effort. All of the training before and after the main lift is set to better improve this movement.

As this book is all about how to improve your Deadlift Max, Deadlifts will always be your main lift for both workouts. One day per week they will be done at a high intensity with low reps to build maximal strength, while one day per week they will be done with a light-moderate intensity as you accumulate volume and practice technique, creating a higher potential for strength gain.

Together, varying between light, moderate and heavy loads will allow for continuous growth without stagnation.

Follow the 12 Week Deadlift Program Chart for your deadlift sets, reps and intensity.

Always warm-up to your working weight slowly during each workout to fully prepare yourself for the work ahead.

OVERLOAD SETS

Overload sets are part of your Main Lift work on Strength Work training days. For this you will either do an AMRAP (as many reps as possible) set or work up to a Daily Max.

Weeks 1-4, 6, 8 and 10 - AMRAP the last set of deadlifts using the same working weight.

For your AMRAP sets, do as many reps as possible minus one. We always minus one because we do not want to ever risk failure. It is better to save some for later, then grind with bad form or risk missing a lift, which stalls progress.

Daily Max

Weeks 5, 7 and 9 - Work up to a Daily Max of 1-3 reps after all your deadlift sets are done.

A Daily Max is a near maximum lift for that given day. It is not a true maximum, because you are fatigued from all the previous work.

For your Daily Max, work up to something heavy, but do not push so hard that you lose technique or risk failure.

Depending on your experience level, you may very well surpass your old max when doing your daily maxes. This is expected and accounted for in the programming. Do not change anything.

DO NOT do any overload sets on weeks 11-12!

Main Accessory Work

Your main accessory is the main accessory lift that directly helps improve your main lift. This lift is included in the 12 Week Deadlift Program Chart on both Strength Work and Base Work training days.

For deadlifts your main accessory is squats and for squats your main accessory is deadlifts.

In any program, you can't talk about deadlifts without talking about squats, and you can't talk about squats without talking about deadlifts. These two lifts work hand in hand to benefit each other. That is why we programmed for both lifts twice per week.

For your squat variation, you can choose anything that works on your weakness in the deadlift. For example, if you have weak quads you should do close stance squats or front squats and if you have weak hips or hamstrings, then do wide stance squats or box squats.

The same goes for your deadlift variation. Choose a variation that works your weakness in the deadlift. If you are weak off the floor, then do deficit deadlifts where you stand on a 1-2 inch mat or plate. If you are weak in the middle or top you can do pause deadlifts where you stop at your struggle point or add bands/chains to the bar. Just don't do anything too crazy, by adding a bunch of variations together. Keep it simple.

Also, your main accessory lift variation can vary every workout or be the same during all 12 weeks.

The idea for this lift is not to overly fatigue you beyond recovery, but rather just hit your muscles from a different angle to stimulate new growth. Just get in some work and do not push too hard. You already did your main strength work. Work the motion with moderate weight and then move on.

Accessory Work

Your accessory work is just a few hard hitting exercises to help build more strength and muscle throughout your entire body. You will be pretty exhausted by this point, but push through and take it as a mental challenge that will make you even stronger.

Your accessory work should be performed with moderate intensity to allow for optimal muscle growth and proper technique. Always maintain good form to ensure proper muscle activation throughout the entire lift.

Focus on stimulating the muscle rather than just throwing around tremendous weight. It is important to always be in control of the weight.

Work every exercise hard and try to move up in weight when you can.

Make sure to finish off with some mobility work to prevent injury.

Strength Workouts

The accessory work for your Strength Work starts off with glute-ham Raises. This is one of the most effective exercises for building brutally strong hamstrings that can support your huge deadlift. If you cannot perform these properly I recommend you start with negatives until you build the strength to do reps on your own.

You can start by kneeling on a pad and having a friend sit on your ankles and descend slowly under control before doing a push up to press yourself back up. When you get strong enough to do these without assistance, your deadlift will likely have shot up significantly by now and you can start holding a weight plate across your chest.

If you do not have a gute-ham raise at your gym, or a friend to help out, you can just do some heavy leg curls instead, but it just won't give you the same results.

Next you will move onto heavy dumbbell rows. Feel free to use straps on these in order to grip heavier weight, but only go as heavy as you can while maintaining proper form. Then pick any bicep curl variation you like before moving onto some side planks and finishing with some mobility work to keep your body injury free.

BASE WORKOUTS

For your Base Work accessories you start off improving your quad strength with the leg press. Do 5 hard sets with moderate to heavy weight and really push your legs to build as much quad strength as possible. This will help both your sumo and conventional deadlift off the floor.

Then you will finish you back work with lat pull-downs before moving onto some curls and weighted planks.

CARDIO/CONDITIONING

Conditioning, or cardio, is not necessary for this program, but can assist with dropping weight and improving recovery, if needed. Just DO NOT do cardio to warm-up!

Conditioning, is any form of work that improves your cardiovascular health and total work capacity while assisting with the goals of training. Some examples of conditioning are; jogging, sprints, jump rope, battle ropes, light circuit training, a daily WOD, sled dragging, or just manual labor.

Conditioning is meant to increase the ability for your body to withstand work and become stronger. If you have low cardiovascular health and little muscular endurance then the amount of work your body can withstand is greatly diminished, along with your ability to become stronger. So, if you have a low work capacity, you should add in conditioning until it improves.

Conditioning can be performed 2-4 times per week for 10-20 minutes at a time. You may utilize high intensity interval training (HIIT) or moderate intensity steady state training.

With high intensity intervals, work to rest should be at a 1:1 or 1:2 ratio. For moderate intensity steady state conditioning, the body should stay in motion throughout the entire time with little to no resistance in order to sustain a raised heart rate during the time used.

It is best to do conditioning immediately after all accessory work, just before mobility work. This will add to the work already done in the workout and allow for the greatest increase in muscular advancement.

Conditioning can also be done on non-training days if preferred, but should then be done for 20-30 minutes. Remember, conditioning is meant to condition your body, not break it down beyond what your body can repair before the next training session. Use relatively light loads and just keep moving.

MOBILITY WORK

Mobility Work is 10+ minutes of stretching at the end of every workout used increase flexibility, prevent injury and improve recovery. Focus on stretching the muscle you just worked, or other tight areas.

It can be as simple as doing just 2-3 stretches for 2 minutes each to fix your elbow, shoulder, ankle, or hip pain.

Mobility work can also be replaced by yoga or any other activity that improves your body's ability to move as intended without pain, such as rolling out soft tissues.

It is best to mobilize right after a workout, but it can also be done on non-training days.

The goal is to get at least 30-40 minutes of mobilization done weekly to enhance your recovery and performance. That is just 10 minutes 3-4 times per week.

REST PERIODS

Rest periods between sets will vary for each part of the workout.

During your warm-up you can superset all your exercises together, as the intensity is not very high for these exercises, or you can take your time with each exercise to prevent fatiguing yourself too much before your main work. It is your warm-up, so do what works best for you.

For all your deadlifts, or main lifts, rest as long as you need between sets, but realize that the longer you take between sets, the longer the workout will last due to the numerous sets.

Typically rest should be 2-3 minutes for loads less than 75% of your maximum and 3-5 minutes for anything heavier. You can take longer if needed, but don't waste all your time waiting to be ready. It is supposed to be hard and tiring, so push yourself and improve your conditioning if needed.

For all accessory work, rest 1-2 minutes between sets.

Training To Failure

There are 2 types of failure in training; technical and absolute.

- **Technical failure** is the point in which you can no longer perform a repetition with reasonably perfect technique. This commonly occurs 1-2 repetitions before absolute failure.

- **Absolute failure** is when no more repetitions can be completed without assistance.

It is good to know what failure feels like, but most of your work should be done with reasonably perfect technique to build the most optimal amount of strength.

You should really only reach technical failure on the last 1-2 sets of any workout, if at all. This means you reached maximal stimuli of the muscle fibers and central nervous system while still performing safe technique.

Reaching absolute failure too often will result in a much greater chance for injury and a much longer recovery period that may extend beyond the next training session. Not only that, but it teaches improper lifting technique as your body fights to lift the weight, and makes you weaker in the long run.

If you are training to failure, then you are training to fail!

The idea for strength training is too, accumulate volume for growth over multiple training sessions per week utilizing perfect practice. This will ensure safety while gaining the most amount of strength over time.

If you do fail

In training, your deadlifts should never go beyond technical failure during this entire program, excluding your Max Day. However, if you ever do fail a rep, then drop the weight by 10% multiplied by the number of reps you have left in your set and do the rest of your sets in shame.

For example, if you failed your last rep, then take off only 10%. If you failed on your 4th rep out of 5, then take off 20%.

If you complete the rest of your sets at this new weight with good form, then you can go back up in weight, but this decreased percentage is your punishment for not recovering properly. Shame on you! Just don't blame me for your lack of preparation.

Also, if the weight is effecting your technique too much and you are moving slow or out of position, then drop the weight by 10-20% until it looks better. It is your job to lift the weight properly and if you cannot do that, then your punishment is lifting lighter weight until you can get it right. Again, not my fault. Just do it right and make it look easy!

- Things are going to go awry and that is ok. Not everything is going to go exactly as planned, and it will take time to perfect your deadlift technique no matter your experience level. Just be patient.

- Just like anything else, whenever you try something new, such as changing your deadlift technique, it will likely feel worse. Your body does not like change and the greater the change the worse things may feel. However, after practicing the new technique you will become so much stronger in the long run. Just trust in the technique and trust in the program. Practice and you will become perfect!

- Don't train lazy! If you do, you will develop bad habits that will haunt you for the rest of your lifting career! Don't squirm when you Bench, sit off to the side when you squat or shrug your deadlifts up. Make sure every rep is absolutely perfect and it will help you during your entire lifting career.

- Recovery is the most important thing! It doesn't matter what you do in the gym; if you can't recover from it, then you are not going to progress. Recovery is the only thing that is going to hold you back from making this program a success. So make sure you are getting enough sleep and fuel! That part is on you.

- Make sure you are doing your *Daily 30* to help with recovery and mobility throughout the entire program.

- Email me (ryan@mathiasmethod.com) with any questions!

- One more thing…

WOULD YOU DO ME A FAVOR?

Thank you for reading and I hope you learned a lot!

Before you go, please do me a HUGE favor and take a moment to let me know what you liked most about this book by leaving a review on Amazon! I read all my reviews and I love hearing how my work has helped others.

Plus, it helps more people learn what they can get from this book!

If you were not completely satisfied with the content of this book please let me know by emailing me directly and I will be happy to answer your questions or help you further.

Thank you, and keep getting stronger my friends!

Email: ryan@mathiasmethod.com

Do you know someone that would benefit from this book?

Please tell them about it!

Everyone can benefit from getting stronger!

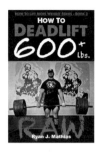

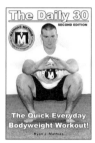

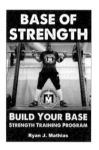

FOLLOW US ON SOCIAL MEDIA

Facebook: @MathiasMethodStrength

Instagram: @MathiasMethod

Twitter: @MathiasMethod

YouTube: @MathiasMethodStrength

Reddit: u/mathiasmethod

FOLLOW THE STRENGTH BLOG

We have over 200+ articles on how to get stronger and workout properly, in and out of the gym!

Go to MathiasMethod.com to follow the Strength Blog and get all the awesome NEW Content we put out!

- **New Articles**

- **Workout Programs**

- **Valuable Strength Training Resources!**

Ironworks Gym

153 South Auburn St.

Grass Valley, CA 95945

PHONE #: (530) 272-9462

Home of the Mathias Method STRENGTH WARRIORS!

Thank you for allowing us to use your awesome facility to help make the world a stronger place!

Strength is only the beginning.

It is what you do with it next that really matters.

Made in United States
Troutdale, OR
07/02/2023

10932842R00057